Feed Me Wicked Things
Juicy Morsels for Gourmands
and Gluttons Alike

by Lee Clark Zumpe

FEED ME WICKED THINGS
BY LEE CLARK ZUMPE

All rights reserved. No part of this book may be reproduced or transmitted in any form or by any means, electronic or mechanical, including photocopying or recording or by any information storage and retrieval systems, without expressed written consent of the author and/or artists.

Feed Me Wicked Things is a work of fiction. Names, characters, places, and incidents are products of the author's imagination. Any resemblance to actual events or persons, living or dead, is entirely coincidental.

Poetry copyrights owned by Lee Clark Zumpe

Cover illustration "Kryvorivnya" © 2015 by Lee Clark Zumpe

Cover design by Laura Givens

First Printing, September 2015
Second Printing, February 2024

Hiraeth Publishing
P.O. Box 1248
Tularosa, NM 88352
e-mail: hiraethsubs@yahoo.com

Visit www.hiraethsffh.com for science fiction, fantasy, dark fiction, and more. Support the small, independent press...

Dedicated to the Librarian—
Thank you for opening the doorway
to limitless worlds

Contents

7	A clutter of whispers
8	Amenemhet
11	Ars moriendi
12	Aegolius funereus
13	Attic Whisperer
15	Catherine's Grave
16	Buryin' Ground
18	Fall River
20	Inexplicable Noise
21	Feed Me Wicked Things
23	Gavrilo
25	In Alignment I
27	In Alignment II
28	In Alignment III
29	October Prayer
31	Kryvorivnya
33	On Crooked River
34	Other Gods
35	Primitive Baptist Church, Tennessee
36	Seven Sisters Mountain
37	Srebrenica
39	The Authors of All Things
41	Subterranean Estates
43	The Black Pond
45	The Blackberry Patch

46	The Deserted Chapel
47	The Oubliette
48	The Lynchin' Tree
50	Victorian Charmer
52	Xenopsylla cheopsis
53	Upon Whose Brow Famine Had Written Fiend

a clutter of whispers

this old house is a clutter of whispers –
a harbor for unrealized dreams,
and a stage for the theatrics of forgotten actors

remote and neglected like the memories
of its former residents, its façade dejectedly
sinks beneath layers of unchecked mold –
its frame buckles and rots from within

anchored to its blackened chambers
and musty corridors,
I am their only audience, now

beside me, the old woman's shadow wilts
like the flowers
I put on her grave last spring

Amenemhet

Where the Bahr el-Libeini canal
curved its course
stretching toward the Fayoum Oasis

the archeologist Maspero
waited for his sun-bronzed laborers
to heave the red granite false door

exposing the descending passageway
leading down a dark corridor
into the belly of the mudbrick pyramid

Amenemhet curved this man's course
stretching his fascination
into obsession

spawning long nights of feverish nightmares
in which he presides over the altar
in the offering hall

where the Nile gods still answer
the whispers of priests
in the Pharaoh's inundated burial chamber

ars moriendi

    She sleeps, now,
while in unseen shadows
haunters wrestle anew;
playing out an ancient allegory
in the quiet graveyards
       of our minds

    She sleeps, now,
while gentle airs soothe
her crestfallen allies:
some spirits' soft ascent
into that dark aether realm
       of tranquil memories

Aegolius funereus

here beneath the Long Night Moon,
weeping shadows form patches of frost –
      and the spirits chafe against the icy gale,
screeching through the boreal owl

I whisper to the anxious twilight
convinced it longs to hear my voice –
      but the spirits chastise me with silence,
binding my soul to this dying winter eve.

Attic Whisperer

On the bitter side of midnight,
amidst the stagnant, apathetic hours
inhabited by inappropriate shadows,
it started mumbling.

At first, so very softly
the winter wind concealed it;
soon it bled into my sleep,
tainting dreams, heralding nightmares.

Speaking some tongue
I cannot consciously identify,
the attic whisperer addresses
something buried in my brain;

some unwanted tenant
squatting in my soul,
suggesting improper things
that haunt me long after I awake.

With each passing night,
the voice becomes more articulate,
increasingly demanding,
progressively persuasive.

Each morning, the unspeakable acts
it advocates seem frighteningly
more horrible, yet horribly
more attractive and appealing.

Catherine's Grave

Astaroth sheds his tears here,
I'm told –
      he pines for you, La Voisin,
and your benefactor the Marquise.
The *chamber ardente*
put an end to your revelry:
Too bad Nicolas found the poisons
in your closet,
the bones in your furnace.
      A candle on your grave
I'm told –
carries a tear-like flame through the night.

Note: Catherine Monvoisin, or Montvoisin, née Deshayes, better known as "La Voisin," was a 17th century French fortune teller, facilitator of black masses and poisoner. She was eventually arrested and convicted of witchcraft. She was burned in public on the Place de Grève in Paris in 1680.

Buryin' Ground

I dig the graves,
look after the grounds;
I lower the dead into the earth
after their loved ones have scattered,
off to feast on gifts of sympathy,
leaving the sweat to me.

I dig the graves:
one size fits all,
ideally,
I don't dislike the job, really,
and when business is slow,
and I have little to do,
I can always help things along –
I don't think that's wrong,
just ambitious.

I'm clean and I'm quick
and true to my keeper:
the reaper never questions
my skills –
though they rest less at peace,
those who I claim:
some nights
I hear their voices as they squirm
clawing at their coffins
and holding back the worm.

Fall River

Late summer in Fall River
beneath the oppressive cover
of Victorian gray skies,
muffled cries precede
silenced testimonies.
  First, there was Abby
facedown between the bureau
and the mattress,
braid severed –
the uninvited stepmother,
alone in the upstairs guest bedroom.
  Next, there was Andrew
in clumsy repose upon the couch
caught napping or unmindful,
shoes dangling –
the credulous patriarch,
alone in the stuffy sitting room.
  And, there was Lizzy
drifting through morphine-blunted denials,
equally bloodless and cold –
the manipulative suspect,
alone with her awful secret.

Late winter in New England
on the banks of the Taunton
where faceless ghosts wander,
silenced appeals rebound
in hushed grave whispers.

Inexplicable Noise

We all hear it. It pulls
us from our dreams, leaving
only a fleeting impression
and an aura of dread. We hear
it, and follows a jumble of
doors ajar, windows cracked,
shadows twitching. We hear
it, and find ourselves as far
from civilization as distance can
accommodate right in our own
neighborhood. We hear
it, and turn to stone. We
hear it, and listen anxiously
until sleep claims us again,
and morning makes us
forget.

Feed Me Wicked Things

Follow me
down a red earth road
in Northern Georgia –

weedy fields
and dark wood
dripping moss –

fill me with loathing
and mistrust,
and fear.

Dump your corpses, here;
hang your troubles
on oak tree limbs,

drown them
in the muddy
swirl of swift creeks:

I crave your sin,
come feed me
wicked things.

Gavrilo

Gavrilo, the diminutive boy from Obljaj,
lingers in an alcove just inside the café,
the buzz of Sunday morning diners
receding like the hungry wails of famished
children late at night.

The opportunity squandered,
he shrivels beneath the weight
of a lifetime of condemnation –
"too small and too weak" to be
of any great consequence.

Along Gebet Street, a fusion of disorder
and disquiet, an unfortunate oversight yields
an unexpected advantage – destiny rarely
allows the luxury of second chances
for those with blind ambition.

A century pivots on one instant:
unlikely assassin, undervalued and
dismissed, only in violence
does he find validation – yet
history reserves no tears for him.

Note: Gavrilo Princip, a Bosnian Serb and Yugoslav nationalist, assassinated Archduke Franz Ferdinand of Austria and his wife Sophie in June 1914 provoking the First World War.

In Alignment
(part one)

Static flesh on unhinged bones
and inert eyes, half-lidded by mold,
mouthful of loam.

Formulae from yellowed page,
vague testaments from another age,
mouthful of Sanskrit verse.

Alien consciousness in imperfect mold,
timeless energy refitting borrowed bones,
sky full of shifting stars.

Author of ancient designs,
distant galaxies willed to align,
sky full of waking gods.

Constellations revised throughout space,
time disfigured, cast out of place,
mouthful of shifting stars.

In Alignment
(part two)

i.
Circling seas of unborn worlds
    orbiting black suns, ignited;
anxious zealots of unborn gods
    by a dark messiah, united.

ii.
Sermons scattered across impoverished
dreams,
eldritch voices taking up new tongues
to sway derelict souls.

Faithless and frustrated and tainted by abuse,
sympathetic hearts quickly succumb
to disgraceful designs.

Untenanted corpses kindled to motion
by the sweetest of wicked whispers
to pledge undying allegiance.

iii.
What happens when our candles wane
    in rising shadows of the night;
What happens when the moon burns red,
    What happens when the stars are right?

In Alignment
(part three)

> Scattered dreams to the stars fly
> To live eternal, though dreamers die.

After life's fitful fever, we idle well
in that hollow womb fit for bones
as the prey of worms and
Servants to the Great Devourer;

yet, quantum loopholes and aberrations
ultimately interrupt our promised peace –
as all sleepers must eventually awaken –
coaxing each soul, each psychic resonance

to drift between islands of galaxies,
ferment in gulfs of Dark Energy,
and fuse with a network of undetectable relations
in the seamless cosmos of indistinct factions.

> When bodies rest in tombs confined,
> Our souls are with the stars aligned.

October Prayer

Early snow above the timberline
and long, insidious shadows
      spilling down the mountain side
      with the touch of frost:
serpentine messengers of harvest-time.

I feel the chill of silenced voices
under bone-white skies like
      pioneer skeletons hidden
      beneath dead leaves
in the sediment of neglected hollows.

The nights stretch like a mortician's arms,
measuring tape eager to size me,
      but I will resist his efforts
      at compulsory relocation;
God willing, the reaper will have to wait.

Kryvorivnya

along ancient footpaths
slithering down the mountain
beneath barren trees
and grave twilit skies,

down to Chornyi Cheremosh
and the Hutsul village
where the ever-winding river
straightens itself.

under the knowing gaze
of impassive stars,
the shadows of ancestors
seethe in alleyways

as Kryvorivnya shudders
in December's embrace,
and a single soul slips
into the dark pit of night.

I watch them succumb –
watch the horse-drawn carriages
carry their coffins
to the lowland cemeteries.

after three hundred years
I still weep as they fall,
as the Ukrainian winter
drains life from their bones.

On Crooked River

Twilight descends on Crooked River,
    darkness swathes the marsh grass,
filters through the surrounding
pine scrub.

I sense the fragile crossing between day
    and night, when witch-fires
glow in the lowlands and graveyards
shudder.

The rustic charm of southern Georgia
    appeals to me no more,
but I am trapped in the serpentine sweep
of the water.

Wormy lungs and a mouthful of mud,
    I have no voice to protest
my unfortunate interment on
Crooked River.

Other Gods

> *Evidence suggests some Picts would cut out the heart of a fierce warrior prior to battle, claiming the sacrifice would induce their war gods to fight alongside them.*
> Heinrich Niemann, **Andre Gotter**

Neither in starry fields of cosmic debris,
Nor in sleeping cities beneath the sea,

Nor in stagnant tombs from forgotten ages,
Nor in moldering tomes between the pages;

Neither frail nor forgotten, nor without goals,
Other gods may employ our unsettled souls;

Neither weakened by time, nor without needs,
These gods may guide our hands and drive our deeds.

Primitive Baptist Church, Tennessee

As I had done for so many years,
I visited Granny's grave in late autumn
a few paces ahead of the snow.
In the old, abandoned church –
perpetually confined
to the shade of solemn white pines –
withered hopes and weary ghosts
stirred whispers in dusty sediment,
shuffling amidst vacant pews.

Standing in the windows,
phantoms whittled from shadow
gazed out across the boneyard.
Oblivious to their ethereal state –
perpetually confined
by the will of dark designs –
I saw them tremble as I faded
amidst those weathered tombstones,
as I had done for so many years.

Seven Sisters Mountain

the fields lay in the gap
on the eastern slope where she
fell off at a slight grade,
where the mountain favored
seasoned settlers;
the forest took it all back, long ago.

opposite the farmlands
on the western side
(looking down over Bone Valley)
the Appalachians wrote another story:
the earth pushed up
silvery yellow slate and flaggy sandstone;

here, the land is steeper
than a mule's face – scoured clean
by cloudburst or hellfire,
a purging of life before our time;
we always kept to our side,
and let the devils have their haint.

Srebrenica, July 1995

with spider-like fluidity
her icy fingers, dancing,
crossing my barren soul,
so delicately,
awoke my flesh
one still night

whispers weaved from shadowy breath
forming a twilight language,
born on nocturnal tongues;
never had such words
fallen from lips
bringing bliss

these lost hearts bound in fierce passion –
these shy immortal lovers –
found brief sanctuary,
a spark of romance,
in the cruel wastes
one still night

dawn brought war to Srebrenica;
in the madness I lost her
and surrendered to dusk…
now, where the dead rest,
I crave one more
burning kiss

The Authors of All Things

Composed of dark matter and mindless faith
    Perched on the rim of the cosmos,
    Tugging at the tapestry
So incomprehensible that neither imagination nor technology
    Can ever hope to discover them
    Or depict their horrible beauty;
These are the authors of All Things with whom we cannot connect,
    Too obscure to be recognizable to their offspring,
    Too insane to recognize their creation.

Subterranean Estates

Beneath a canopy of mourning oaks
dangling Spanish moss like ladies'
tear-stained kerchiefs,
the shadow-haunted stones stagger
in weedy abandon,
bowing drunkards tottering with age,
chipped and cracked –
some altogether capsized
and facedown against the gorged earth,
upset and terminal in frozen grief.
Patches of moss highlight the epitaphs
of their neglected lodgers,
and clumps of withered flowers
in sun-blanched vases
echo forgotten prayers softly whispered.
Beneath the fading footprints
of departed caretakers,
embracing their independence,
the dead amuse themselves
as best they can
in the wormy shallows
of their subterranean estates.

The Black Pond

I awoke from a deep sleep,
Startled by some strange yet familiar noise.
Too shaken to slip back into slumber,
I found my coat and gloves
And ventured out into the cold December
    evening.
I stepped quietly
Down the old carriage road
Under the winter-weary branches
Of somber balsams.
Little mounds of dirty snow
Sulked along the path.
As the gray, pitching sky descended
And wicked, icy fingers of wind
Stroked the tree tops,
I came upon the black pond.
It was smaller than I remembered;
To any boy, though, it was an ocean.
In the summers of my childhood,
We came here.
I and my two brothers
Spent long August afternoons
In the cool waters
While the sun lingered above the crest
Of Old Sugarloaf
Waiting for us to grow tired.

It seemed darker now,
Though I always knew it held secrets.
I eased down to the shore
Where the icy surface of the dormant pond
Kissed the cold, wet ground.
Anxious, I leaned forward
And sought my reflection.
Gazing back at me, over my shoulders,
I saw them.
Paul and Erik, grim-faced, gaunt,
With hollow cheeks and pursed lips,
Stood there, frozen like the water,
Their eyes pleading.
And as I watched, entranced,
Their hands came up,
Their twisted fingers
Slithered down over my shoulders:
They wanted me to join them.
I stood --
Shook off the apparitions
And dismissed the past.
I retreated from the black pond
And made my way back up the carriage road.
Not until I was a good distance away
Did that infernal noise cease;
How I loathe that sound they always make
When their fingers scrap and claw at the
bottom of the ice.

the blackberry patch

now, down in the hollow,
nothing but palpable dusk:
      shards of Erebus
sprinkled amidst the hemlock and spruce

and a two-story stone chimney
abandoned to the wilderness,
      splotches of moss
gradually scaling the shaded tower

and a coal black cauldron
deserted near the fire ring:
      tangle of residue,
decomposing into anonymity

now, down in the hollow,
nothing but unmarked graves:
      piles of bones,
clutching fingers in the blackberry patch

The Deserted Chapel

The dark wood reclaims it
bit by bit, year by year:
tuliptrees settle in the adjacent field,
serpentine roots embracing
the cold gravestones.
Dewberry vines cloak the front steps,
blackberry brambles
skirt the rickety split-rail fence,
and mud daubers whirl through
the stagnant air above the pulpit.
Sometimes the shadows come
to drift amidst the pews,
and some nights the dusk
erupts with lightning bugs
as though the black-veiled minister
who perished long ago
might still perform candlelight vigils.

the oubliette

white bones suspended in
descending coils:
perpetual agonies
pooled in stagnant shadow
      hovering
above petrified death throes

from the oubliette
only an occasional complaint:
sporadic whimpers tinted gray
      with age,
and shallow disembodied whispers

The Lynchin' Tree

When they built the courthouse
        during Reconstruction,
that old oak already had a reputation.

Now, some folks used to post bulletins –
        nail 'em right to the trunk,
legal notices, wanted posters and such.

Might be mentioned that in its shade
        plantation owners once gathered,
inspecting new shipments from African shores.

And then there was Augustus:
        a mob dragged him from the jailhouse,
set him to swinging for something next to
nothing.

Been four summers since lightning struck it,
        its twisted branches blackened
and leaves scattered like severed digits.

Dead and rotted, they cut it down –
        But when the moon wills it,
I still see the shadow of the lynchin' tree.

Victorian Charmer

skirted by rose bushes, lilacs
and a host of venerable perennials
      it squats atop the mossy crag
      arching over the harbor

glowering over the town, its
apathetic turret ringed by sea fog
      on autumn evenings
      framed by shrieking gulls;

black cats curl into shadows, dust
settles upon deserted wood floors
      and weeds sprout
      amidst the garden stones

and on certain nights, when
moonlight floods the mansion
      the old man comes back
      and stares out the window.

Xenopsylla cheopsis

the fleeing Genoese packed up their troubles
        and made for Italy; little did they know
the horrors their flight would spawn.

on Mediterranean shores, Messina bowed
        first – its streets flooded with forsaken
corpses,
its halls peppered with cowering survivors;

fever, convulsions, and shock followed by
        disseminated intravascular coagulation:
dark skin at the extremities, Black Death.

blight of the scroungers, bloodsucking
        rat-riders, scavenging the countryside
leaving mass graves and chaos in their wake.

Upon Whose Brow Famine Had Written Fiend

She shrank away into a corner
of the unfurnished apartment,
her shadow getting leaner
everyday;
the darkness at night
bit into her flesh,
each morning she seemed
more pallid,
more feeble.

In her youth,
she had been a beauty –
of that, there was no doubt:
the boys would linger
on the front steps
waiting to light her cigarette
or smell her perfume;
she found she could live
off smiles and innocent kisses
for a while –
eventually, they wanted
more.

But the dark days
took all the boys away,
and the old men had
no spare change
for her;
one harsh winter
robbed her of all that beauty.

Now she sits
and waits for another
caller to appear on the steps.

About Lee Clark Zumpe

Lee Clark Zumpe, an entertainment columnist with Tampa Bay Newspapers, earned his bachelor's in English at the University of South Florida. His nights are consumed with the invocation of ancient nightmares, dutifully bound in fiction and poetry. His work has been seen in magazines such as *Weird Tales*, *Space and Time* and *Dark Wisdom*, and in anthologies including *Horrors Beyond*, *Corpse Blossoms*, *High Seas Cthulhu* and *Cthulhu Unbound Vol. 1*.

Lee lives on the west coast of Florida with his wife and daughter.

Visit him at www.leeclarkzumpe.com.

www.ingramcontent.com/pod-product-compliance
Lightning Source LLC
LaVergne TN
LVHW012054070526
838201LV00083B/4669